Project 7-11

Developing Science

Godfrey Hall

for 8-9 year olds

Letts

1 Soapy problems

"This soap isn't very good, is it?"

"That's because we're using cold water."

You will need:
- a half-filled washing-up bowl
- a bar of soap
- liquid soap
- washing-up liquid
- different types of material, e.g. cotton, wool nylon
- orange squash
- a teaspoon

▶ Collect together your pieces of material.
▶ Put a teaspoon of orange squash on the piece of cotton and wash it in cold water.
▶ Now try the same thing with a piece of wool and then the nylon.
   Which was the easiest to get clean?

▶ Record your results in your notebook.

"Here is a test to see how well soap works."

▶ Get a bowl of water.
▶ Put a teaspoonful of orange squash on your hands.
▶ Wash your hands using only the water.

▶ Now get another bowl of cold water.
▶ Put the same amount of orange squash on your hands.
▶ This time, wash your hands using the soap.
   Did the squash come off more easily when you used soap?

Try to make sure that you use exactly the same amount of soap each time and also that you rub your hands together the same number of times for each test.

▶ Repeat this test using warm and then hot (but not too hot) water.

> Write your results on the chart.

Water	No soap	With soap	With washing-up liquid
Cold			
Warm			
Hot			

▶ Now do the test again using washing-up liquid.

▶ Record your results. Is washing-up liquid any better than soap for washing your hands?

> Here's a test using liquid soap.

Try washing four dirty plates or cups.

▶ Wash one in hot water and one in cold water.
▶ Then wash the other two, one in hot water and one in cold water using liquid soap.
Try to be fair by using the same amount of liquid soap and rubbing each plate in the same way.

▶ Record your findings in your notebook.

2 Helicopters and all that!

▶ Collect together some seeds and leaves. Drop them to see how they fall.

Here is a way of making your own helicopter.

You will need:
- a piece of stiff card
- glue
- a pair of scissors
- a ruler
- a pencil

Look at those seeds. They look just like helicopters.

▶ Cut out two pieces of card 12 cm long and 3 cm wide.
▶ Glue them together in the shape of a cross.

▶ Now hold your helicopter at the end of one of the strips and flick it into the air.

How did it come down when it was flicked?

▶ Record what happens in your notebook.

▶ A second way to launch your helicopter is to hold it in the middle and throw it straight up into the air.

Do you notice any difference in the way it travels through the air?

▶ Record your results.

Which was the best method of launching your helicopter? Was it the first or the second way?

Can you think of any reason for this?

As you flick it, do you notice that it rotates just like the blade of a real helicopter?

▶ Try launching your helicopter into the wind and with the wind. Watch what happens.

> If the wind gets under your helicopter, it will lift it higher and higher!

▶ Try using different shaped pieces of card and bend them in different ways. Does this improve your helicopter?

3 Making a magnet

You will need:
- a magnet
- a needle or pin
- an iron nail
- a cork
- a dish with some water in
- pins or paper clips

You can make a magnet quite easily.

▸ Take a needle or a pin and stroke it with a magnet.
Make sure that you stroke your needle or pin in the same direction each time.
Be careful not to bang the needle.

▸ See how powerful your magnet is by counting how many pins or paper clips you can pick up with it.

You can increase the power by stroking it some more times with your original magnet.

▸ Fill in the chart below.

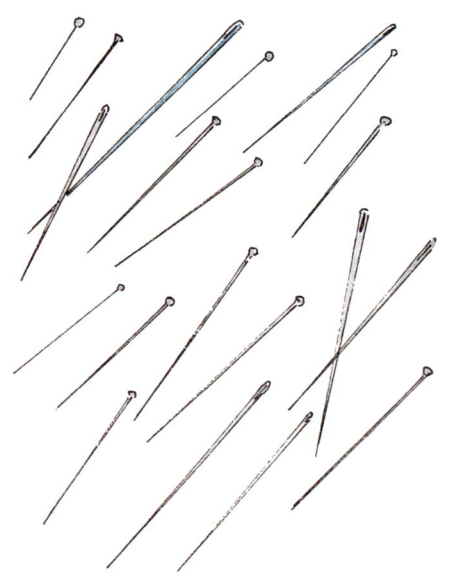

Number of strokes of the magnet	Number of pins or clips it held
10	
20	
30	
40	
50	

▶ Try making a nail magnet.
▶ Stroke a nail with your real magnet.

Remember to use an iron nail.

▶ Leave it for a few days and then test to see if it will still pick up any paper clips.

▶ Leave it for some more days and test it again. Does leaving it make any difference to its strength?

Warning ▶ **Ask an adult** to bang your nail really hard with a hammer. Does this make it lose its magnetic power?

It's quite easy to make a compass using your needle magnet.

▶ **Ask an adult** to cut the cork.

▶ Lay your needle magnet carefully on top of it.

▶ The needle should point north!

▶ See if you can find any magnets around your home that perhaps do not look like magnets at all.

You may be able to find some that close doors such as the fridge or kitchen cupboards.

Perhaps you have some stuck on to the outside of the fridge to keep notes on?

▶ Make a list in the box opposite of any that you find.

4 Hovering hovercrafts

"Did you know that the rubber thing around the bottom is called a skirt?"

"It doesn't look much like a skirt to me."

▸ Put a piece of paper on the table and blow underneath the paper. Watch what happens.

▸ Try this out with a number of different shaped pieces of paper and see if the different shapes make any difference to the way it moves.

What happens as the air gets under the paper?

You will need:
- a piece of stiff card
- a pencil
- a pair of scissors
- several pieces of paper
- sticky tape

"Here is a way to make your own hovercraft."

▶ Take a piece of card and draw along the lines as shown below.

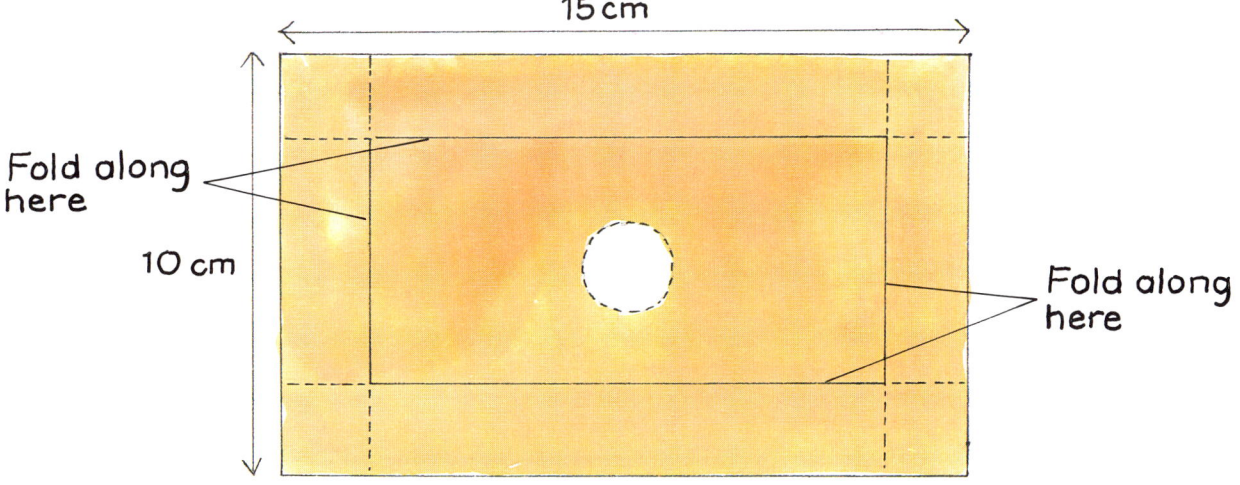

▶ Cut a small circle from the middle.
▶ Cut along the dotted lines and fold the card under to make a shallow lid or dish.

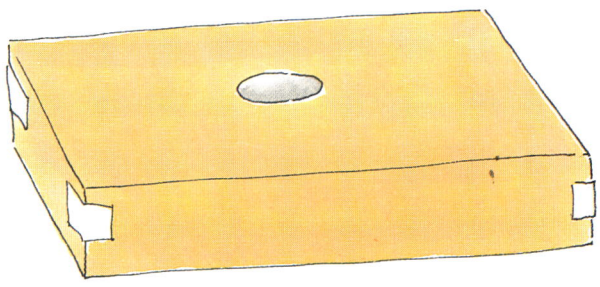

▶ Stick the corners down with tape.

▶ Roll up a piece of card into a tube.
▶ Glue or tape the edges then push the cardboard tube through the hole.

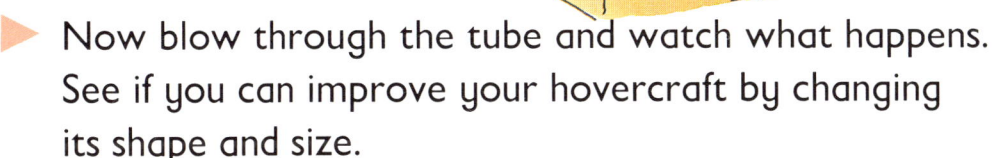

▶ Now blow through the tube and watch what happens. See if you can improve your hovercraft by changing its shape and size.

▶ See if you can find and draw a picture in your notebook of a craft that could move across the surface of the water in a different way. It could be a jet ski, a hydrofoil, or a jetfoil.

5 Music makers

Can you make any sounds by cupping your hands together and blowing through them?

"This makes a brilliant sound. Listen!"

One way of making a simple sound is to get a comb and put a piece of tissue paper over it.

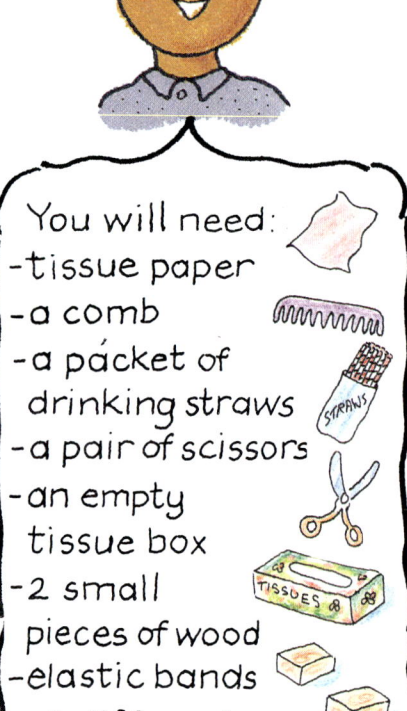

You will need:
- tissue paper
- a comb
- a packet of drinking straws
- a pair of scissors
- an empty tissue box
- 2 small pieces of wood
- elastic bands of different thickness

▶ Blow through the paper and see what kind of sounds you can make.
▶ Try out different types of paper until you find the best sound.

Which type of comb is best?
▶ Try ones with teeth close together and ones with teeth further apart.

"You could also try plastic and metal combs."

Here is a musical instrument made from a drinking straw.

▶ **Ask an adult** to cut the end of a straw and make it into a point.

▶ Now flatten the point with your fingers.
▶ Hold the straw between your fingers and blow through it with the pointed part in your mouth.

What kind of sound does it make?

▶ **Carefully** cut off the other end of the straw.
See if it makes any difference to the note. Is it higher or lower?

▶ Make some more pipes of different lengths. See what kind of sounds they make.

> Be careful not to make the straws too short.

▶ **With an adult**, cut some holes in your pipes and see if they make any difference to the sound.

Another instrument that is easy to make is this guitar.

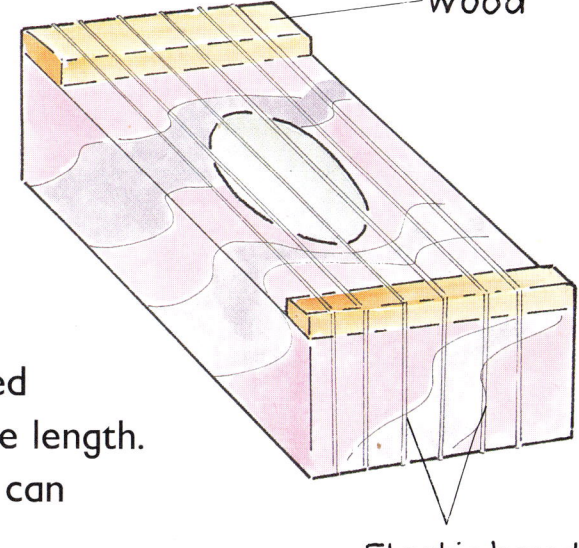

▶ Put the two pieces of wood on the top of the tissue box.
▶ Now stretch your elastic bands around the wood and the box.

▶ Make sure that the bands are firmly fixed and of different thicknesses but the same length. They should be well spaced so that you can pluck them easily.

> Which bands make the highest sounds: the thick ones or the thin ones?

6 Digging about

Have you ever noticed what happens when the ground is dug up and left?

▶ Look at a piece of freshly dug garden or park after it has rained. See if any of the soil has been washed on to the path or into a gutter.

▶ Look carefully at the soil in the gutter. Has anything happened to it?

Here is one way of looking at soil.

You will need:
- 2 or 3 plastic lemonade bottles
- some water
- an old teaspoon
- a magnifying glass

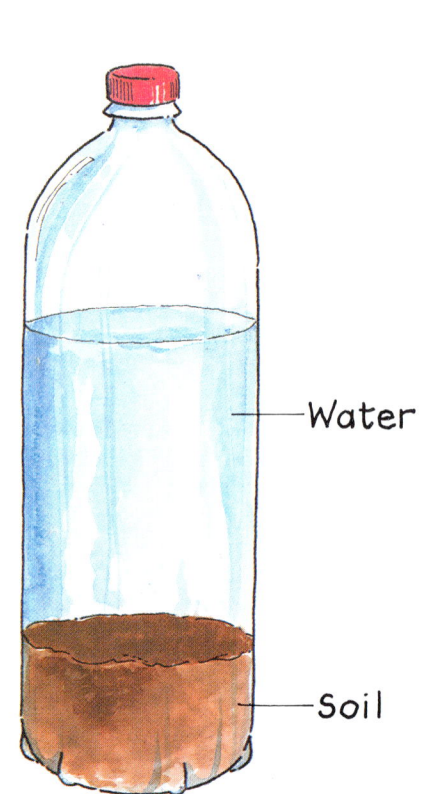

Water

Soil

▶ Take a clear lemonade bottle and put three or four tablespoons of soil into the bottle.

▶ Fill the bottle with water until it is three-quarters full.

▶ Screw on the top, making sure that it is tight.

> Give the bottle a good shake.

▶ Leave the bottle until the soil has settled.
What do you notice about the soil?
Is there anything floating on the top?

▶ Now try the same test using some different soil.
Can you see any difference when the soil has settled?

▶ Fill in the bottle chart below showing what happened in each of your tests.

Test 1   **Test 2**   **Test 3**

▶ Go out after it has rained and see if you can find any small rivers of water and soil.

▶ Have a look at the stones and soil through your magnifying glass and see what they look like.

7 Skating on water

Pond skaters can often be seen on ponds or stretches of still water. They don't sink because they skate across the surface of the water.

You can show how this works yourself.

You will need:
- a clean glass
- washing-up liquid
- a pin or needle
- a paper clip
- a used match

▸ Fill a clean glass with water. Make sure it is full to the brim.

▸ Look through the side of the glass. What do you notice?

Do this very carefully.

▸ Very gently, lay a pin or needle on the surface of the water and watch what happens. Make sure you drop it flat on to the water without piercing the surface.

▸ Look through the side of the glass again. What do you notice now?

▶ Now try the same test using other objects such as a paper clip, or a used match.

▶ Write down in your notebook what happens to them and why you think they float or sink.

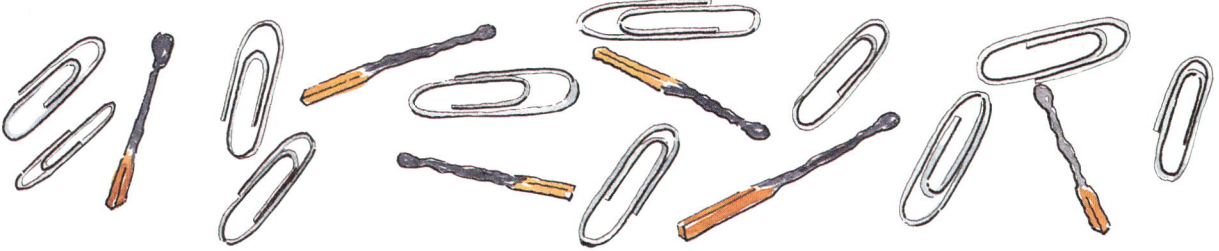

▶ Use the space below to draw a picture of what you see.

▶ Float your needle on the surface of the water.

▶ Carefully drip some washing-up liquid into the water. What happens?

▶ Try other liquids, such as lemonade.

▶ Make a note of what happens.

Did you know...?

The pond skater can stand on the surface of the water because of something called **surface tension**.
The pond skater's legs press into the surface of the water but bend it rather than break it.

8 Keeping a diary

> How much time do you spend watching television every week?

> I'm not sure – about two hours a day, I think.

You will need:
- a notebook
- a pencil
- crayons or felt tips

It is often a good idea to keep a record or diary of what you have done or seen over a period of time.

Here are one or two ideas you could try.

▶ Keep a record of some of the television programmes that you watch every day over a period of a week.

▶ Fill in the chart below.

Day	Date	Starting and finishing times	Title	How long it lasted

▷ Put a star by the programmes that were entertaining and a tick by the ones that helped you to learn something.

▶ Take a small notebook and go through it writing Monday at the top of the first page, Tuesday at the top of the second, and so on.

Here are the days of the week to help you: Monday, Tuesday, Wednesday, Thursday, Friday, Saturday, Sunday.

▶ Repeat this through the book until you have written on every page.

▶ At the end of each day write down some sentences about what you have done during the day.
In the same diary you could also keep a record of what the weather is like.

▶ Every day you need to go outside and see what kind of day it is.

▶ Then fill in your day as shown below.

You could make up your own pictures.

You could also write down if it is **hot, warm, cold, very cold** or **freezing**

Other things you can write about in your diary are people you meet, places you visit and any unusual things that happen.

There have been some very famous diary writers. Can you find out their names and what they wrote about?

9 In a minute!

What can you do for one minute?

You will need:
- a digital watch or timer
- a pencil
- a piece of paper
- a small bouncy ball

▶ Get two or three friends together and see how many times they can write their names on a piece of paper in one minute.

▶ Record the results in your notebook. Why do you think this test might be unfair? Is there any way in which you could improve it so that everyone has a fair chance?

▶ Write down a list of what else you think you could do in a minute. How many times can you jump into the air with both feet together? How many times can you clap or bounce a ball?

Try to make your tests as fair as possible and have a guess at how many times you think you can do it before you try it out.

You can make your own chart for your results or you can use the one on the page opposite.

Jumping into the air		
Name	**Guess**	**Result**

▶ Get a friend or an adult to check your results.
You could use the same sort of chart for clapping or bouncing the ball.

> Make your tests as fair as possible.

▶ Now try the same test over a period of four or five minutes and record your results below.

Name	Jumping into the air				
	Minutes				
	1	2	3	4	5
Kim 3.00			✓		✓
Rebecca 8.15			✓		✓
Lindsey					

What do you notice is happening as the minutes go by?
Why do you think this is?

> Guess how long a minute lasts – without looking at a watch or clock.

▶ Get someone to time you. Tell them when you think you've reached the end of your minute.
How close were you? If you have several turns, do your results get better?

10 Shadowplay

▶ Find a darkened room. Switch on your torch and put your hand in front of the beam. A shadow will form on the wall.

▶ Watch what happens when you move the beam of light to one side.

▶ Go outside on a sunny day.

▶ Push your stick into the grass or a pot of soil so that 20 centimetres are showing.

▶ Mark where the end of the shadow is. Do this every hour. What do you notice? When do you get the shortest shadow? Can you think why this happens?

▶ Fill in on the chart below the length of your shadow at certain times during the day.

You will need:
- a torch
- a pen for marking
- a cane or stick 25 cm long
- a tape measure

Now see if you can find out when you get the longest shadow.

Time	Length of shadow
9am	
10am	
11am	
12 noon	
1pm	
2pm	
3pm	
4pm	

▶ Try making the same shadow clock on another day in the year.
How long are your shadows now?
Why do you think there is a difference?

▶ Find out how many hours of daylight there are on certain days in the year.

> Do you know why there is more daylight in summer than in the winter?

▶ Draw a picture of a sunny day in summer showing short shadows.

Summer

▶ Now draw another picture showing a winter's day with long shadows.

Winter

Try testing out shadows on different coloured backgrounds.
Does the colour of your shadow change depending on the colour of the background?

11 Watching worms and woodlice

You will need:
- a plastic see-through container with lid
- earth
- a trowel or small fork
- a magnifying glass
- kitchen towel
- a piece of wood or bark
- stones
- dead leaves
- cling film or polythene
- a spoon
- shallow box

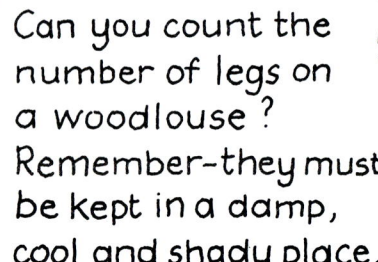

Can you count the number of legs on a woodlouse? Remember – they must be kept in a damp, cool and shady place.

Worms are interesting creatures – did you know that there are thirty different kinds to be found in Britain at the moment?

Woodlice are also good creatures to study. They have flattened bodies and a tough shell. They can be found in damp and shady places such as under logs or stones.

▶ See if you can find any worms or woodlice. Try looking in the soil under trees or under stones.

▶ Pick them up gently with a spoon, and place them in a container with some damp soil.

▶ Write down in your notebook the differences between a worm and a woodlouse.

**Always be very careful when you handle your minibeasts.
Wash your hands after touching them.**

Here are two ideas for observing the worms or woodlice you have found.

Worms

- Fill your plastic sweet jar or container half-way up with soil and punch some small holes in the lid.
- Make sure your soil is damp. Put in your worms.
- Keep a record over the next few days of what they do.

Woodlice

- Find a shallow box or container and line it with kitchen towel or blotting paper. Make sure that it is damp.
- Now collect a piece of wood or bark for your woodlice and put in a few large stones, together with some dead leaves or soil.
- Cover the top with some polythene or cling film.

> Make sure that you prick some holes in it so that they can breathe.

- Put your woodlice in their new home and guess what they will do.
- Check to see if you are right.

Do you think that they will go to sleep at night?

- Keep a record of what they do over the next few days and then return your creatures to their homes **carefully**.

12 Doing it with mirrors

Be careful when you use a glass mirror.
When you look into a mirror you see a **reflection** of yourself.

▶ Look into a mirror and draw a picture of yourself.

You will need:
- a small mirror
- a torch
- a ball that bounces
- salt or pepper pot
- a tablespoon

▶ Look around the house and make a list of the different mirrors you can find. Are they all the same kind?

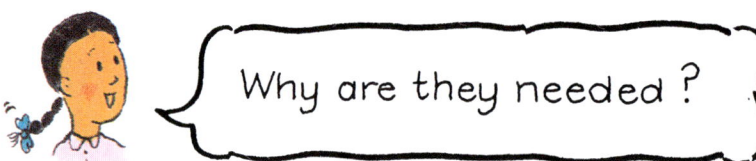

Why are they needed?

▶ Find somewhere dark and point your torch at the mirror.
▶ Switch it on.
▶ Write down what happens when you shine the torch into the mirror.

Can you see how it is reflected in the mirror?

▶ By shining the beam into the mirror, see if you can move the beam around the room as it is reflected.

▸ Look at your reflection in the tablespoon. What do you notice?

▸ Now turn the spoon over and look again.

▸ Draw what you can see in each spoon in the spoons below.

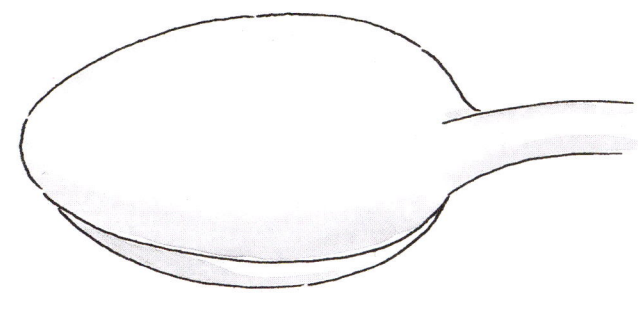

What do you notice is different?

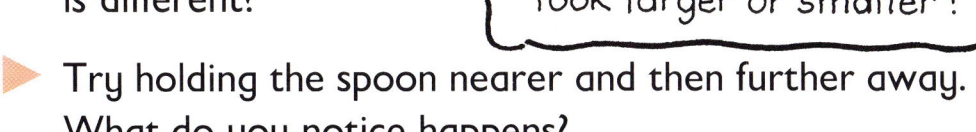
Does the spoon make you look larger or smaller?

▸ Try holding the spoon nearer and then further away. What do you notice happens?

▸ Now try some other spoons of different shapes and sizes.

Some mirrors can make you look larger and some can make you look smaller.

▸ Take the salt or pepper pot and put it in front of a small pocket mirror.

▸ Move the mirror to the left.

▸ Now move it to the right. What is happening to the reflection?

▸ Get someone to sit down opposite you. Pretend that they are the reflection in a mirror.

▸ See if you can move your hands at **exactly** the same time as your partner.

▸ Now swap over and you can be the reflection.

It's more difficult than it looks!

13 Watching it rise

"I wonder if we could make some bread?"

You will need:
- a wooden spoon
- a mixing bowl
- a measuring jug
- 1 level teaspoon of salt
- 1 level teaspoon of sugar
- 2 level teaspoons of dried yeast
- 450g of plain flour
- a greased tray
- 360 ml of warm water
- a damp tea-towel

Here is a simple recipe for making your own bread.

▷ Wash your hands and put on an apron.

Warning — **Get an adult to help.**

▷ Mix the flour and salt in a heatproof bowl.

▷ (Keep a small amount of the mixture separate from the rest and use this to make some bread without yeast.)

▷ Put the bowl in a warm oven for about 10 minutes.

▷ Put some of the warm water into the jug and mix in the sugar and yeast.

▷ Stir once and leave for about 10 minutes until there is a good froth on the top.

▷ Make a dip in the bowl of flour. Add the yeast mixture.

▷ Mix it in with the wooden spoon. Add the rest of the water.

▶ Mix up the dough with your hands until there are no more bits on the side of the bowl.

▶ Sprinkle some flour on to a clean surface. Take the dough out of the bowl.

▶ Fold it in half and keep folding and pressing until it is no longer sticky.

▶ Cut up the dough into 12 pieces and roll each piece into a ball.

▶ Put these on a greased tray. Sprinkle them with a little flour.

▶ Cover the tray with a damp tea-towel. Leave it in a warm place for up to an hour.

▶ Now take off the tea-towel and see what has happened.

▶ **Ask an adult** to put your dough into a preheated oven at 220°C or gas mark 7 and bake for 10 minutes.

▶ **Ask an adult** to take one out and put the rest back into the oven for another 10 minutes.
What do you notice about the one you have just taken out?

Let them go cold before you eat them!

What happened to the bread you made without using yeast?

14 Cloudy weather

If you look up into the sky you can sometimes spot all sorts of different clouds. Be careful not to look directly into the sun.

▶ See if you can draw some of the different shaped clouds in your notebook.

If you look up you may be able to spot some very high clouds or some lower down that look like cotton wool.

▶ Look very carefully at the clouds and see if any of them are grey or black. What do you think this means?

Is it going to rain or is it going to be fine?

Draw a picture showing a fine day with a clear sky or just a few white clouds. Then draw a stormy day with grey or black storm clouds.

Clouds are made up of millions of tiny water droplets that are so light they float in the sky.

When the air cannot hold them any more they fall as rain.

Here are some names of different types of clouds.

Stratus

Cirrus

Cumulus

Nimbostratus

▶ Fill in the chart below by drawing in some of the clouds you see.

Day	Type of cloud	Name
Monday		
Tuesday		
Wednesday		
Thursday		
Friday		
Saturday		
Sunday		

15 Static electricity

When some people comb their hair they produce **static electricity**. This is electricity that does not move.

You can often make this kind of electricity by rubbing things together.

You will need:
- 2 or 3 balloons
- plastic combs
- tiny pieces of paper
- a woolly jumper
- a long cane or stick

▶ Comb your hair or rub the comb on a woolly jumper.

▶ Hold it next to some tiny pieces of paper. Watch what happens to the paper.

The comb attracts the paper.

▶ Blow up a balloon. Rub it against a woolly jumper several times and then press it against the wall.

Watch what happens!

If this doesn't work too well, use a different jumper or try again on another day.
Choose a day when the air is dry. Cold winter days are sometimes the best.

▶ Try out your comb and balloon on other materials and see what happens.

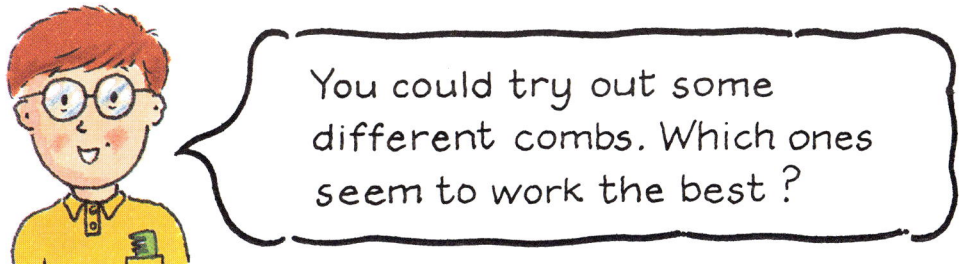

You could try out some different combs. Which ones seem to work the best?

Here is another idea you might like to try out using static electricity.

▶ Tie two balloons on to a long, thin cane or stick, next to each other.

Make sure that they are touching.

▶ Rub each of the balloons against the woolly jumper. Watch what happens.

▶ Try brushing newly washed and dried hair in front of a mirror in a completely darkened room.

▶ Record your findings in your notebook.

▶ See if you can pick up any other objects with your 'charged' comb. You can always 'recharge' it by rubbing it against the wool.

▶ Hold the comb at different distances from the objects. Does this make a difference?

Chart showing National Curriculum attainment targets together with topics covered

	Exploration of science	Variety of life	Processes of life	Genetics and evolution	Human influence on earth	Types and uses of materials	Making new materials	How materials behave	Earth and atmosphere	Forces	Electricity and magnetism	Information technology	Energy	Sound and music	Light/electromagnetic radiation	Earth in space	Nature of science
Soapy problems	●					●											
Helicopters and all that	●									●							
Making a magnet	●										●						
Hovering hovercraft	●									●							
Music makers	●													●			
Digging about	●								●								
Skating on water	●					●				●							
Keeping a diary	●		●													●	
In a minute!	●			●								●					
Shadow play	●															●	●
Watching worms and woodlice	●	●	●														
Doing it with mirrors	●															●	
Watching it rise	●					●							●				
Cloudy weather	●								●							●	
Static electricity	●										●						